om

WILLIAM COLLINS SONS & CO LTD
London Glasgow Sydney Auckland
Toronto Johannesburg

First published 1980
© Elizabeth Walter, 1980
ISBN 0 00 216 728 X

Designed by Trevor Vincent
Made and printed in Great Britain by
W. S. Cowell Ltd, Ipswich

*The illustrations of Victorian and Edwardian cards and
scraps are reproduced by courtesy of Ronald Clark,
The Mansell Collection, The Victoria & Albert Museum and
Yvette West.*

SEASON'S GREETINGS

Compiled by

ELIZABETH WALTER

MAY · FORTUNE

FAVOUR · YOU
IN · EVERYTHING

COLLINS
St James's Place, London
1980

NEW YEAR

Here we bring new water
From the well so clear,
For to worship God with
This happy New Year.
Sing levy dew, sing levy dew,
The water and the wine,
The seven bright gold wires
And the bugles they do shine.

Sing reign of Fair Maid
With gold upon her toe,
Open you the West Door
And turn the Old Year go.
Sing reign of Fair Maid
With gold upon her chin,
Open you the East Door
And let the New Year in.

This Welsh New Year song refers to the old belief
that the first water drawn from a well on New Year's
Day had special cosmetic and healing properties.
There was keen competition to be the first to draw it.

Among his other activities Julius Caesar reformed the Roman calendar and created a new month in the depths of winter. He named it after the god Janus whose feast occurred at this time. Janus was the god of beginnings, always a hazardous time. He was depicted with two faces, one looking forward, one back. Busts of him were placed over doors to keep out evil.

SNOW

January brings the snow,
Makes our feet and fingers glow.

Whirling white snowflakes look like feathers. So 'the Old Woman is plucking her geese' or 'shaking her featherbed' are two old explanations for falls of snow.

The scientific one is that snow results from precipitation of water vapour into solid crystals at temperatures below freezing. Snowflakes form lacy hexagonal crystals, no two alike. They may mat together to form larger flakes if the snow descends through a layer of warmer air.

Nothing is quite so quiet and clean
As snow that falls in the night,
And isn't it jolly to jump from bed
And find the whole world white? . . .

And while we are having breakfast,
Papa says, 'Isn't it light?
And all because of the thousands of geese
The Old Woman plucked last night.'

from SNOW IN TOWN *by* Rickman Mark

PLOUGH MONDAY

The first Monday after January 6, the end of the Christmas season, was called Plough Monday because it was the day when work started again on the farms, and – weather permitting – the spring ploughing began.

In some rural areas this old tradition is now commemorated on the first Sunday after January 6 instead. It is known as Plough Sunday. A plough is brought into church and blessed, and prayers are offered for a good harvest.

With what content and merriment
Their days are spent, whose minds are bent
To follow the useful plough.

OLD SONG

February brings the rain,
Thaws the frozen lake again.

Which accounts for February's nickname: February fill-dyke.

The name February comes from Februa, the Roman festival of purification which took place during this month, but some have thought it derives from the Latin word for fever – *febris* – since fevers were also common at this time. Certainly the fever known as 'Spanish influence', or *influenza*, is rife this month.

If the weather is mild in February the blackthorn or wild plum may blossom. The white flowers appear before the leaves on the black branches: hence the name blackthorn. The cold spell which often follows is known as the blackthorn winter.

CANDLEMAS DAY

If Candlemas Day be fair and bright
Winter will take another flight.
If Candlemas Day be cloud and rain
Winter is gone and will not come again.

OLD RHYME

Candlemas Day – February 2 – takes its name from the blessing of candles on this day for use in church throughout the coming year. It is the Feast of the Presentation of Christ in the Temple, when Simeon hailed him as 'a light to lighten the gentiles', and also of the Purification of the Virgin Mary.

Candlemas is the last day of the extended Christmas season, when any greenery not taken down on Twelfth Night (January 6) was removed and the Yule Log was burnt for the last time.

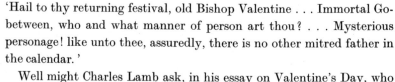

ST. VALENTINE'S DAY

'Hail to thy returning festival, old Bishop Valentine . . . Immortal Go-between, who and what manner of person art thou? . . . Mysterious personage! like unto thee, assuredly, there is no other mitred father in the calendar.'

Well might Charles Lamb ask, in his essay on Valentine's Day, who the Immortal Go-between was! Very little is known about him. He was a priest of Rome or a bishop of Terni – the two may even be identical. Both were martyred in the third century on February 14, after lives of exemplary chastity, and neither has any connection with lovers. The connection is thought to lie in the date, which fell on the eve of the Roman festival of Lupercalia when numerous fertility rites took place.

A valentine is an anonymous declaration of love sent on this day to the person of one's choice, either in the form of a gift or of a card copiously adorned with hearts, flowers and lace. The valentine should arrive in the morning – afternoon is too late. Occasionally the valentine may be the admirer himself – or herself. Shakespeare refers to this in *Hamlet*:

> *Tomorrow is St Valentine,*
> *All in the morning betimes,*
> *And I a maid at your window*
> *To be your valentine.*

A delightful belief without the least foundation is that the birds choose their mates on this day.

SHROVE TUESDAY

Shrove Tuesday, the day before the beginning of Lent, gets its name from the custom of going to confession on that day and being shrived in preparation for the long period of fasting and abstinence ahead. It is perhaps even better known as Pancake Day. Since eggs and fat were not eaten in Lent during the Middle Ages, they all had to be used up, and pancakes are the traditional way of doing so. They must be tossed, of course; turning them won't do.

Shrove Tuesday, Ash Wednesday, when Jack went to plough,
His mother made pancakes, she didn't know how.
She tossed them, she turned them, she burned them quite black,
She put in some pepper and poisoned poor Jack.

OLD RHYME

LEAP YEAR

February 29 occurs once every four years. Leap years have existed since the days of the Ancient Egyptians, for although there are 365 days in the calendar, it actually takes $365\frac{1}{4}$ days for the earth to return to the same position in relation to the sun. To keep in step with the extra day thus created, a day was added every fourth year. When the Romans revised the Ancient Egyptian calendar, they added the extra day to February because it was the shortest month.

A Leap Year can only occur at the turn of the century if the year is exactly divisible by 400. So the year 2000 will be a Leap Year, the first since the year 1600.

In Leap Year a woman may propose to a man – but only if she is wearing a red flannel petticoat.

March brings breezes loud and shrill,
Stirs the dancing daffodil.

March comes in like a lion and goes out like a lamb.

March is named for Mars, the Roman god of war. It was the first month of the Roman year, and the planet Mars is appropriately the ruler of the sign Aries, the Ram, the first sign of the Zodiac, which the sun enters this month.

March is traditionally the windy month, gales being especially frequent around the spring equinox (March 21), when the hours of daylight and darkness are equal.

Children who pull faces are in danger during March. If the wind changes while they are doing so, they will be unable to change back.

ST. DAVID AND ST. PATRICK

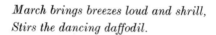

St David (St Dewi) is the patron saint of Wales, and founder of the see of St David's, where he presided over the abbey for many years. His feast day falls on March 1 and the first daffodils are said to bloom in his honour.

His other emblem is the leek – the sixth-century abbot-bishop is supposed to have lived for some time on bread and leeks, and possibly this association sanctified the plant. The Welsh are said to have been wearing leeks when they won a famous victory over the English in the seventh century, and this further enhanced the plant's properties in their eyes. It is still worn by the Welsh regiments on St David's Day.

St Patrick is the patron saint of Ireland. His feast day is March 17. He was the son of a fourth-century christianized Roman Briton and at the age of sixteen was carried off by pirates from his coastal home and enslaved in Ireland, where he worked as a herdsman. Six years later he escaped, but after he reached home he was recalled to Ireland in a dream to preach the Gospel. This he did so successfully that by AD 444 he was able to establish his see at Armagh. The Archbishop of Armagh is still the Primate of All Ireland.

St Patrick's emblem – and the emblem of Ireland – is the shamrock. He allegedly used the three-leaved plant to illustrate the mystery of the Trinity.

March

MOTHERING SUNDAY

In an age of few holidays, the middle Sunday in Lent was one when young people working away from home were given the day off to visit their mothers. The traditional gift was a Simnel cake.

I'll to thee a Simnel bring,
'Gainst thou goest a-mothering,

wrote Robert Herrick in the seventeenth century. The commonest form of Simnel is a rich fruit cake

with a layer of marzipan in the middle and another on top.

Mothering Sunday is not identical with Mothers' Day, an American festival occurring on the second Sunday in May and first established in 1914, largely through the efforts of a Philadelphia lady who had recently lost her own beloved mother and wished to see all mothers honoured.

LADY DAY

Lady Day – March 25 – is the day of the Annunciation by the Angel Gabriel to Mary: Our Lady's Day. No one knows when the Annunciation actually took place, but when Christmas Day was fixed on December 25 in the fourth century, the Annunciation naturally fell into place nine months before the supposed birthday of Christ.

Lady Day is one of the four quarter days in England, Wales and Ireland when quarterly payments fall due. The others are Midsummer (June 24), Michaelmas (September 29) and Christmas Day. Scotland has its own quarter days.

From the twelfth century until 1752, when England abandoned the Julian calendar, the year was officially reckoned to begin on Lady Day. Accounts closed two weeks later. So the end of the financial year is still April 5, and the usual date for the Government to present its Budget is the Tuesday immediately after.

MARCH HARES

No wonder the Mad Hatter had tea with a March Hare in Lewis Carroll's *Alice in Wonderland:* they were two of a kind. Hares were thought to be mad in March because these normally shy animals could be seen leaping and boxing in the fields by moonlight. In fact it is the mating season, and the gymnastics are part of the mating dance.

Fortunately the hares recover their sanity by Easter, because these animals are the traditional bringers of children's Easter eggs, although in recent years the hare has been increasingly replaced by the commoner Easter Bunny.

April brings the primrose sweet,
Scatters daisies at our feet.

The name April comes from the Latin word *aperire* –
to open, because it was the opening of the year.

The robin and the redbreast,
The robin and the wren,
If ye take out of their nests,
Ye'll never thrive again.

The robin and the redbreast,
The martin and the swallow,
If ye take out of their nests,
Bad luck will surely follow.

The four popular birds mentioned in this old rhyme were once held sacred : the robin because his red breast associated him with fire and light, and later with Christ's blood which stained his feathers when he hopped on the Cross; the wren because he is the King of All Birds, having won the contest to see who could fly highest by hiding unnoticed in the eagle's feathers (an early example of a booster missile?); and the martin and the swallow because they signified the return of summer.

Many people still consider it lucky to have a swallow's or martin's nest on the house.

APRIL FOOL

'He who hath not a dram of folly in his mixture, hath pounds of much worse matter in his composition.'

from ALL FOOLS' DAY *by Charles Lamb*

April 1 is All Fools' Day – the day when the practical joker is in his element and the air is loud with cries of 'April Fool!' Of course the joke must be played before noon, otherwise it rebounds on the joker and he is the April Fool.

No one knows the origin of this spring custom, but the fact that the joker's licence ceases at noon suggests a survival from some ancient ritual perhaps once associated with a pagan feast. The custom is known all over the English-speaking world, and in some European countries as well.

MAUNDY THURSDAY

The name Maundy derives from the Latin word *mandatum* – commandment. It was the first word in the antiphon for the day and referred to the washing of the feet of the disciples by Christ. In remembrance of this, specially minted Maundy money is presented by the Sovereign to as many poor elderly men and women as there are years in the Sovereign's life. This replaces the earlier custom of washing the feet of thirteen poor men.

The rose is red, the violet's blue,
Sugar is sweet, and so are you.
These are the words you bade me say
For a pair of new gloves on Easter Day.

The rhyme is a reminder that gloves were once the traditional Easter gift.

Easter is the feast of the Resurrection of Our Lord, but the word Easter derives from Eastre, a Saxon goddess of spring. It is a movable feast because it occurs on the Sunday following the first full moon after March 21, the spring equinox. So the earliest possible date is March 22, which last occurred in 1818 and will next occur in 2285, and the latest date is April 25, which last occurred in 1943 and will not happen again until 2038.

Eggs are an essential part of Easter. They symbolize renewed life and were an important part of pagan spring festivals long before Christianity. The early Christians adopted them as symbols of the Resurrection and exchanged them as gifts at Easter. Boiled eggs still appear regularly on Easter Sunday breakfast tables, and egg rolling takes place in numerous districts, including Washington DC, where the President of the United States traditionally rolls an egg on the White House lawn.

ST. GEORGE

St George for merry England!

How St George came to be the patron saint of England is a mystery. The soldier-saint never set foot here, but it seems likely that returning Crusaders established his cult, for from very early times he was venerated in the Holy Land, where he was probably martyred about AD 300.

No historical details of his life are known. There is, alas, no evidence that he ever killed a dragon or rescued a maiden; these details occur only in late versions of the legends surrounding him. Indeed, he is so vague a figure that in 1960 he was demoted by the Roman Catholic Church.

Nevertheless, he remains the patron saint of England and of the Order of the Garter, and his badge of a red cross on a white ground flies from church towers and public buildings on national occasions, and on his feast day of April 23.

May brings flocks of pretty lambs,
Skipping by their fleecy dams.

Sheep huddling together is a sign of rain, but the shepherd
had other means of forecasting the weather:

If the evening's red and the morning grey,
That is the sign of a bonny day.
If the evening's grey and the morning red,
The lamb and the ewe will go wet to bed.

And the bee-keeper could begin to estimate his wealth:

A swarm of bees in May
Is worth a load of hay.
A swarm of bees in June
Is worth a silver spoon.
A swarm of bees in July
Is not worth a fly.

May takes its name from Maia, a Roman fertility goddess
and the daughter of Atlas, who bore the world on his shoulders
and has since given his name to a book of maps of the world.
Maia was also the mother of Mercury, the messenger of the gods.
The planet Mercury is the ruler of the sign Gemini, the Twins,
which the sun enters this month.

MAY DAY

Come, lasses and lads,
Get leave of your dads,
And away to the maypole hie.

OLD SONG

The many country ceremonies connected with May 1 are the last vestiges of pagan fertility rites to welcome the spring. Yet the best-known – dancing round the maypole and crowning the Queen of the May – are deliberate nineteenth-century revivals. Flowers, including the may (hawthorn) itself, have always played an important part in the celebrations. 'Here a boy gathering lilies and lady's-smocks, and there a girl cropping culverkeys and cowslips, all to make garlands suitable to the present month of May,' wrote Izaak Walton in *The Compleat Angler* in the seventeenth century. The Romans held the festival of Flora, goddess of flowers, for several days around May 1.

Since 1889 May Day has also had an urban significance. In that year the Second Socialist International designated it a holiday for radical labour. May Day parades are held in a number of Socialist and Communist countries.

WHITSUN

Spring goeth all in white,
Crowned with milk-white may:
In fleecy flocks of light
O'er heaven the white clouds stray.

White butterflies in the air;
White daisies prank the ground:
The cherry and the hoary pear
Scatter their snow around.

ROBERT BRIDGES

Whit Sunday, the seventh after Easter, is the day of Pentecost when the Holy Spirit manifested itself to the Apostles. The name Pentecost comes from the Greek word for fiftieth, because it is the fiftieth day after the Jewish feast of the Passover.

In the early Church it was a favourite time for new converts to be baptized, and the name Whitsun – White Sunday – is supposedly a reminder of the white robes worn by the converts for the occasion.

June

June brings tulips, lilies, roses,
Fills the children's hands with posies.

June is thought to be named for the goddess Juno, wife of Jupiter,
or just possibly for the great Roman family of Junius.

Roses are inseparable from June, and the rose is the emblem of England. Originally it was a royal badge, but ever since Henry VII created the Tudor rose by blending the red rose of Lancaster – he was connected with the house of Lancaster – and the white rose of his wife, a princess of the house of York, it has been our national flower.

Although the finest roses came from the East (returning Crusaders brought back the rose of Damascus, known to us as the damask rose), the wild rose seems to be a native of these shores. The Roman naturalist Pliny the Elder, AD ca. 23-79, even speculated that the old name for England, Albion, might be derived from the white rose, *Rosa alba*, which grew here in profusion when the Romans came.

MIDSUMMER DAY

June 24 is Midsummer Day, when the sun reaches its highest point in the heavens. It is also the feast of the Nativity of St John the Baptist, a much honoured saint in the early Church. The date of his birth, like Christ's, is conjectural, but the summer solstice was chosen because it enabled the Church to christianize the various pagan fire ceremonies held at that time. These were now claimed to be in honour of the Baptist's birth. In some parts of the country bonfires still blaze on the hilltops on June 24.

To most people, however, Midsummer is associated with the faery world. Oberon and Titania lead the revels, Puck plays his pranks, and the short night is filled with dew and gossamer and banks 'whereon the wild thyme blows', just as Shakespeare made it in *A Midsummer Night's Dream*, a play which incorporates many of the sixteenth century's beliefs about fairies.

July

Hot July brings cooling showers,
Apricots and gillyflowers.

Thunderstorms are common in July but we no longer use them to fore-tell the future in the manner Leonard Dygges describes in *Prognosti-cations* (1555):

'Thunders in the morning signify wind; about noon, rain; in the evening, great tempest. Some write (their ground I see not) that Sunday's thunder should bring the death of learned men, judges and others; Monday's thunder the death of women; Wednesday's thunder the death of harlots and other bloodshed; Thursday's thunder plenty of sheep and corn; Friday's thunder the slaughter of a great man and other horrible murders; Saturday's thunder a general pestilent plague and great death.'

Julius Caesar renamed the months of his reformed calendar, which is why the names have Roman derivations. He named July after himself because he was born this month.

ST. SWITHIN'S DAY

July 15 is St Swithin's Day. He was a bishop of Winchester in the third century. When he died, he asked to be buried in the churchyard where the rain could fall upon him, and this was duly done. Some years later it was decided to accord the bishop more honourable burial within the cathedral, and July 15 was the date appointed for his bones to be moved. But it rained so heavily on that day that removal was impossible. The bishop was thought to be showing his displeasure – and his displeasure lasted for the next forty days. This is the origin of the rhyme:

St Swithin's Day, if thou dost rain,
For forty days it will remain.
St Swithin's Day, if thou be fair,
For forty days 'twill rain nae mair.

THE DOG DAYS

The Dog Days, the period of greatest heat, run from approximately July 3 to August 11, that is, twenty days before and twenty days after the conjunction of Sirius, the Dog Star, and the sun, as originally calculated in Mediterranean countries.

Sirius, the brightest fixed star in the sky, is in the constellation of the Dog (Canis Major).

Dogs were thought particularly likely to go mad during this time of sultry heat. A popular cure for the bite of a mad dog was to make the victim swallow several of the animal's hairs. Hence the saying, often quoted by those who have over-indulged, 'a hair of the dog that bit,' indicating the belief that a little more of the same can do no harm.

CHERRY RIPE

Cherry ripe, cherry ripe, ripe, ripe, I cry,
Full and fair ones, come and buy.

Herrick's poem, better known as a song (it was set to music in the eighteenth century by the English composer Dr Thomas Arne), repeated the cry of the street-vendors of this most popular fruit.

The finest cherries came from Buckinghamshire, particularly around Stowe, and were made locally into turnovers known as

cherry bumpers. The first Sunday in August, which marked the end of the cherry-picking season, used to be known as Cherry Pie Sunday.

Cherry bounce was a popular Victorian drink made from cherry juice, sugar, spices, brandy and rum. It was bottled, kept well, and must have been extremely potent.

Riddle me riddle me rote-e-tote,
A little wee man in a little red coat,
A stick in his hand and a stone in his throat,
Riddle me riddle me rote-e-tote.

Answer: a cherry

August

August brings the sheaves of corn,
Then the harvest home is borne.

The corn dollies, made to traditional designs and now available in many craft shops, are the last survival of a very old custom. They were made originally from the corn of the Last Sheaf left standing in the middle of the field, last refuge of the Corn Spirit. Whoever cut the Last Sheaf killed the Corn Spirit, and ill luck attended him. To spread the ill luck as widely as possible, the reapers threw their sickles in turn at the Last Sheaf, so that all contributed to its downfall.

The corn dolly was taken back to the farmhouse in procession – the Harvest Home – and presided over the Harvest Supper. It was then kept until the following year, when a new one replaced it.

Since Julius Caesar had named July after himself, his successor, Augustus Caesar, named the month following after *him*self. But at that time August had only thirty days, whereas July had thirty-one. Determined not to be outdone, Augustus is alleged to have taken a day from February and added it to August. Which is why February has only twenty-eight days.

AUGUST BANK HOLIDAY

Come unto these yellow sands,
And then take hands.

Every year, thousands of people accept at least the first line of Shakespeare's invitation. A seaside holiday, at home or abroad, is still the favourite, even if it is only a day trip on August Bank Holiday.

Four public holidays, when banks closed and therefore no business could be transacted, were instituted in 1871. They were purely secular, but the first three – Boxing Day, Easter Monday and Whit Monday – were added to religious festivals. Then came August Bank Holiday, the first Monday in August, which gave everyone another long weekend, culminating for many in 'a day at the sea'.

In 1971 August Bank Holiday was changed to the last Monday in August to shorten the long period without a holiday between the beginning of August and Christmas. At the same time Whit Monday disappeared, to be replaced by the last Monday in May, which only rarely coincides with Whitsun, and two new bank holidays were added: January 1 and the first Monday in May.

Warm September brings the fruit,
Sportsmen now begin to shoot.

Since the Roman year began in March, September was the seventh month.
It takes its name from the Latin *septem* – seven.

Apples ripen this month, the fruit of temptation, whether to small boys scrumping in orchards or to Eve when offered the Forbidden Fruit by the Serpent in the Garden of Eden. But there is nothing in the Bible to suggest that the fruit was an apple, and figs, dates and oranges have all been put forward as contenders for this doubtful distinction. Sir Thomas Browne, writing in the

BONHEUR A TOI!

seventeenth century, suggested that the apple was the likeliest because it was also the commonest, although the word for apple in Greek could equally well mean an orange, a lemon or a quince.

Far from Pomona, the Roman goddess of gardens and orchards, giving her name to the apple, she probably acquired hers from it: *pomus* is the Latin for apple.

HARVEST MOON

The great gold lantern of a moon hung low in the sky which we associate with the time of harvest festivals is the Harvest Moon, the full moon occurring nearest to the autumnal equinox (September 21). Because the angle of the moon's path to the horizon is minimal at this period, the moon rises at the same time for several nights in succession, instead of fifty minutes later each night, as normally. Consequently the moon appears to hang low in the sky for a longer period, making the early evening light.

The same applies to the full moon following, which is known as the Hunter's Moon.

MICHAELMAS

St Michael's feast occurs fittingly at the beginning of winter, when the days grow shorter and darkness encroaches on light.

The traditional English food for Michaelmas was a goose, because spring goslings became ready for table at this time.

Michaelmas (Michael's Mass) is today best known in connection with the garden daisies that bloom in September, with the autumn term at Oxford, and as one of the four quarter days.

September 29 is the feast of St Michael the Archangel, the only angel to be so honoured in the Western Church. Michael was believed to be the leader of the heavenly host, who personally hurled the rebellious Lucifer from Heaven down to Hell. He was therefore considered particularly adept at ousting devils, and churches dedicated to him were often on the site of pagan temples. Such temples were frequently situated on hilltops, which explains Michael's association with high places, although the most famous, Mont St Michel off the coast of Normandy, was founded as the result of a vison of the saint vouchsafed to a tenth-century local bishop.

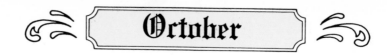

Fresh October brings the pheasant,
Then to gather nuts is pleasant.

October, the eight month of the Roman year, takes its name from *octo* – eight.

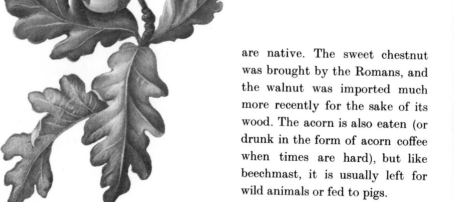

Nuts are a valuable if neglected food, though not necessarily a slimming one: one pound of kernels can contain up to 3000 calories.

Four edible varieties of nut grow in Britain: hazel, sweet chestnut, beech and walnut, though only the hazel and beech are native. The sweet chestnut was brought by the Romans, and the walnut was imported much more recently for the sake of its wood. The acorn is also eaten (or drunk in the form of acorn coffee when times are hard), but like beechmast, it is usually left for wild animals or fed to pigs.

Hallowe'en (October 31) is the eve of All Hallows, hallows being an old world for saints and saints having been honoured on November 1 ever since the ninth century. It is also the old New Year's Eve of the pagan Celts, for their year began on November 1, the feast of Samhain. At that season the dead were supposed to revisit their homes, so Hallowe'en has always been associated with ghosts.

Since the dead were feared and their ghosts regarded as evil spirits, all those who trafficked with them were active at this time, and October 31 was one of the great witches' sabbaths, the other being April 30, May Eve, or Walpurgisnight. So owls, bats, broomsticks and black cats are part of our Hallowe'en decorations, and games of fortune-telling are rife.

Nuts and apples often play a part in these games. Bobbing for apples in a tub of water does not offer a peep into the future, but if the apple peel be removed in one long strip and thrown over the left shoulder, it will form the initial of the future spouse. And if a girl sit alone and veiled before her mirror at midnight with a single candle burning, she will see reflected in the glass the face of her future husband looking over her left shoulder while the clock strikes twelve.

Dull November brings the blast,
Now the leaves are falling fast.

The name November comes from the Latin *novem* – nine.

It is traditionally the month of fogs.

> *No sun, no moon,*
> *No morn, no noon,*
> *No dawn, no dusk,*
> *No proper time of day,*

as Thomas Hood somewhat negatively described it in the last century.

By contrast, it is also the month of St Martin's Summer, the period of fine weather which often occurs around November 11, the feast day of the Roman soldier-saint who is usually depicted in the act of cutting his cloak in half to share it with a beggar.

This respite before the onset of winter is also known as the Halcyon Days. A halcyon is a kingfisher, recalling the Greek maiden Alcyone who was so happy with her husband that she dared to compare them to Hera and Zeus. For this presumption the gods drowned Alcyone's husband, and when she flung herself into the sea after him, both were transformed into kingfishers.

Kingfishers choose their mates at this time of year, which is named in their honour, but a period of calm, mild weather occurring at any time is often referred to as 'halcyon days'.

GUY FAWKES DAY

'Penny for the guy!' Not all the children who hump round a masked effigy and collect pennies in the weeks preceding November 5 have any idea who Guy Fawkes was.

This Roman Catholic gentleman of good Yorkshire family was discovered in the cellars of the House of Commons on November 5, 1605, the night before the State Opening of Parliament. With him were thirty-six barrels of gunpowder and a long, slow-burning fuse which would enable him to escape before King, Lords and Commons were blown sky high. In the resulting confusion Guy Fawkes and his fellow conspirators intended to seize power and restore England to the Roman Catholic faith. The plot failed and the conspirators, including Guy Fawkes, were executed. Ever since, his effigy has been burnt on a bonfire on the anniversary of his capture, to the accompaniment of fireworks and much jollification.

The bonfires were originally part of the traditional Hallowe'en celebrations, but were easily transferred to the slightly later date. The popularity of Bonfire Night continues undiminished among children.

Please to remember the fifth of November,
Gunpowder Treason and Plot,
I see no reason why Gunpowder Treason
Should ever be forgot.

CHILDREN'S RHYME

THE LORD MAYOR'S SHOW

Turn again, Whittington,
Thou worthy citizen,
Lord Mayor of London.

The Dick Whittington who heard the message of the bells and turned back really existed, and so perhaps did his cat. At any rate, a Sir Richard Whytyngdone was Mayor of London three times: in 1397, 1406 and 1419, and rode in procession through the streets of the City.

The Lord Mayor's Show on the second Saturday in November is the last surviving pageant of the City of London, when the new Lord Mayor drives in state from the Mansion House, his official residence, to the Royal Courts of Justice in the Strand, where he is sworn in. The first recorded mayor of the City was elected in 1209, King John agreeing to his election by the fiercely independent City provided he came to present himself to the Sovereign or his appointed ministers at the palace of Westminster. This is the origin of the procession.

From the mid-fifteenth century until the Royal Courts of Justice were opened in 1882 the procession went by water in decorated barges. The Lord Mayor's gilded coach was built in 1757 to take the Mayor from the Mansion House to the wharf where he embarked. It cost £860 and was paid for by the City aldermen. Today it takes him on a longer route, and except for its annual day of glory, it is on show in the London Museum.

ST. ANDREW

How did St Andrew, a fisherman of Galilee and the first called of the Apostles, become the patron saint of Scotland? He preached the Gospel in Greece and Southern Russia, of which countries he is also the patron saint, and was martyred in Asia Minor, allegedly on an X-shaped cross. His bones were transferred several times before finding a final resting-place in Amalfi Cathedral in Southern Italy.

But legend has it that some of his bones were brought to Scotland in the fourth century. A Greek abbot named Regulus is said to have been visited by an angel who commanded him to take the saint's bones, sail westward with them, and then build a shrine wherever he should chance to come ashore. Regulus did so, and landed eventually at what is now St Andrews on the coast of Fife. The shrine he built is covered by the site of the cathedral.

St Andrew's Day is November 30.

Chill December brings the sleet,
Blazing fire and Christmas treat.

December was the tenth month of the Roman year and takes its name from the Latin word for ten – *decem*.

Perhaps it is better if December does bring sleet and snow in view of such cheerful statements as 'Green December fills the graveyard,' or:

If Christmas Day be bright and clear
There'll be two winters in the year.

White Christmases, however, seem to be getting rarer. Before the calendar change in 1752, when Christmas Day fell on what is now January 6, they were more common because snow often reaches England in the first half of January. Since the beginning of this century there have been only seven Christmases when snow has fallen in London, and only three of these have given the city a Christmas-card appearance: those of 1927, 1938 and 1970.

FATHER CHRISTMAS

Father Christmas does well to have a long white beard: he is one of the oldest and most English figures connected with the festive season and survived even the attempts of the Puritans to suppress Christmas.

'Sir Christmas', as he was often called, never had any religious associations. These belong to St Nicholas, the original Santa Claus, whose feast day falls on December 6, the day when many European children receive their gifts. But St Nicholas was a bishop of the early Church; consequently he was not one of the select band of saints still honoured by the new Church of England, and the Puritans, of course, looked askance at all saints, so he never became popular in England. But 'Sir Christmas' persisted among country people, and even figures in one of Ben Jonson's court masques of the early seventeenth century. Gradually he became the very embodiment of the Christmas spirit, and when the cult of Santa Claus arrived from the United States in the last century, the two soon became fused.

Father Christmas traditionally wears a long red robe with a fur-trimmed hood, whereas Santa Claus wears tunic, breeches, boots and cap.

The term 'Father' was simply an honourable form of address for an old man, as in Father Time. There has never been a Mother Christmas.

A Mer